1

A Redhead

Looks at

60

by,

Joan Ellen Gage

A Redhead Looks at 60

Copyright 2015 by Joan Ellen Gage

DEDICATION

I dedicate this book to my paternal Grandmother, Laura Higley Gage and to her daughter, my aunt, Dorothy Gage Favitta.

I thank them for their influence on my life as strong and creative women.

Table of Contents

5

6

Introduction

In this book, I have written several poetic messages, many of them with a comedic edge. This is my third book and I've taken it up a notch with more photos creations which serve as the spice in the "recipe!" I hope you enjoy the humor and the inspiration. Rock on!

9

"If you are always trying to be normal, you will never know how amazing you can be."

--Maya Angelou

I HAVE TRIED THEM ALL!

A Redhead Looks at 60

With Apologies to Jimmy Buffett

(Tune—A Pirate Looks at 40)

I've slathered on the lotion; I've played hard ball,

trying to capture my long-lost youth

from the shops at the mall,

I've tried them all, I've tried them all.

Fought to stop the weight gain, watched it fall and rise,

when I put those blue jeans on,

I think I'm in disguise,

can't trust those thighs, can't trust those thighs.

I'm turning 60 in just a few days.

I'm not sure how I got here,

but I think I'm OK.

I've got to stop wishin', complainin' and bitchin,'

and try to embrace the day.

I'm well on my way, come what may.

I'm well on my way, come what may.

We've just got today;

don't throw it away.

We've just got today;

don't throw it away.

Don't Desert Yourself

Yea though I walk through

the desert of my past

criticizing what went wrong

and if only I hadn't said or done that

We can't go back and fix these events

they are carved in stone

all we can repair is our attitude toward ourselves

and move on

We need to give our inner children

some tough love

encourage them to grow up and out of the past

and into the now

Carpe Diem

ELISA--READY
TO MOLT!

15

Stranger in a Strange Skin

I feel foreign in

my flesh. Who is

that in the mirror, peering out

of my eyes?

I cannot disregard the feeling that

there are two of us, one

old familiar self and

another who is either molting my

skin or making a pupa out of it!

The latter would be better, as

I would emerge svelte and energetic, a

doppelganger of my former self! I realize

that this is another passage,

16

I've enjoyed all of them. This

one makes me suspicious, it

whispers to me of more

wrinkles, aching joints, etc., the

coming attractions—

not very attractive to me!

Still, here we are, in our prime, and

starring in our own sequels. How

cool is that?

Acceptance

It's the hardest thing a woman can

do to accept herself as she is, faults and all, and

rise above Western civilizations' criticism.

Our society has created a model, that

few can touch: ultra-thin, flawless,

plus, giant breasts, based

on the Barbie doll figure.

Women come in all shapes and sizes, each

perfect in their own way. We must

find our own exquisiteness, and

embrace and love ourselves, our

unique and wonderful selves!

Creeping Toward 60

I am trying to reconcile myself

with myself,

not sure who I'm becoming, or

where the journey will take me.

That 50/60-something person morphing

into an unrecognizable flesh, foreign

yet undeniably mine. It's that

contents shifting thing, the

DNA rearranging a bit.

I confess I thought some of the body changes would

come later, much later. We

are easily duped into thinking this, when

women with perfect skin and bodies,

peer out from our magazines.

I feel a bit deceived, actually, fifty

felt and looked so good on me. Of course, that

was before the menopause fairy

bopped me on the head with her aging wand!

Being estrogen-less is a mixed blessing, but

I'll take it. As the

older folks love to say,

"Beats the alternative!"

Wadda You Want—a Medal?

Women are hard working.

They work out of the home, in the home,

around the house, around the clock.

Without so much as a thank you,

women keep it going, encouraging one another,

or pitching in to help as needed.

Let's give ourselves

the recognition that we deserve,

be our own cheerleaders, and fan clubs.

Don't give up—stand proud,

and say it with feeling—out loud,

"I'm a wonderful woman, and I rock!"

EMBRACING
YOUR INNER
HIPPIE!

By
Jean Ellen Gage

Author of :
Water Running Downhill!
Words of Empowerment for
Women in Midlife

70's Interlude

Caught in rare daydream, old rock tunes pumping

out of the garage radio below, drifting in--

Baby I Love Your Ways, transports me. I am in the 70's,

wearing cut off patched jeans, braless, alive, free,

my beautiful soul still unmarred,

pupa to butterfly stage nearly complete,

venturing out onto the planet of free love,

with Boone's Farm Strawberry Hill nights.

Inhaling music as oxygen, learning

new secrets in the dark.

That girl is still within me, I

feel the bitter sweetness of that

innocence mixed with my life's experience,

a harder heart carrying many scars, but capable

24

of great levels of love and compassion.

I try to conjoin us, to fuse the two into one,

where we can be at peace and forgive one another.

The past's bad relationships, and low self-esteem,

stemming from fear and anxiety, has

hobbled us for so many years. I

pray for us, for this healing, with my

heart expanding with gratitude and love.

Namaste

These Times Are a-Changing

The decades are rolling by. My 20's

were a timid adventure; by 30, I thought I knew it all.

My 40's were rocking; I was finally getting it together.

50 struck and I was awed at how fabulous life was,

I learned to take time to breathe and to create.

60's are different; at least the prelude seems to be.

This decade has caused me to think more frequently

about the effects of aging and to ruminate on that.

But, I'm sure I'll find my balance again, and

come to terms with life's sneaky body changes.

This will come with prayer and meditation,

plus, the support of all my wonderful friends.

I salute them and love them—awesome women!

May we all soar with each other's help, Amen.

Arise from Your Ashes

The dream is still alive and waiting. It

waits for you to restore it to wholeness, and

inhale life into the

very lungs of hope, to

deliver the kiss to your

sleeping beauty heart's desire.

The time has come to break into the

vault of your psyche and

free the urn of creativity,

turning life's ashes into a new vision.

Come unearth your treasure; stake

your claim, rediscover your destiny. Join me,

arise from your ashes, rise up; be reborn!

DEBBIE FULLY BAKED!

HALF BAKED

What is it with families?

We're weird patchwork quilts

of our ancestor's traits.

Each of us put together

a little differently, but

we've got the same genes.

Genes that have wonderful DNA, and

others that showcase all that

crazy, like the OCD one, or

the control gene.

We're all part of the same batch.

Like cookies, some families

just have more fruit and nuts!

Future Vision

I want to live in a society,

where varicose veins rock, and

flabby thighs are sexy.

Where the more chins you have,

the more you are admired.

I want to live in a society,

where moving up a size is envied, and

throngs of women want to know,

how did you do that?

I want to live in a society,

where the deeper the lines on your face, the

handsomer the women look, and

the grayer your hair is,

the more enlightened you appear.

But mostly, I want to live

in a society, where kindness abounds.

Where you are accepted, loved

and treasured as you grow older.

This is what we all deserve.

Let us not judge one another harshly, and

be who we were born to be—

awesome, pass it on!

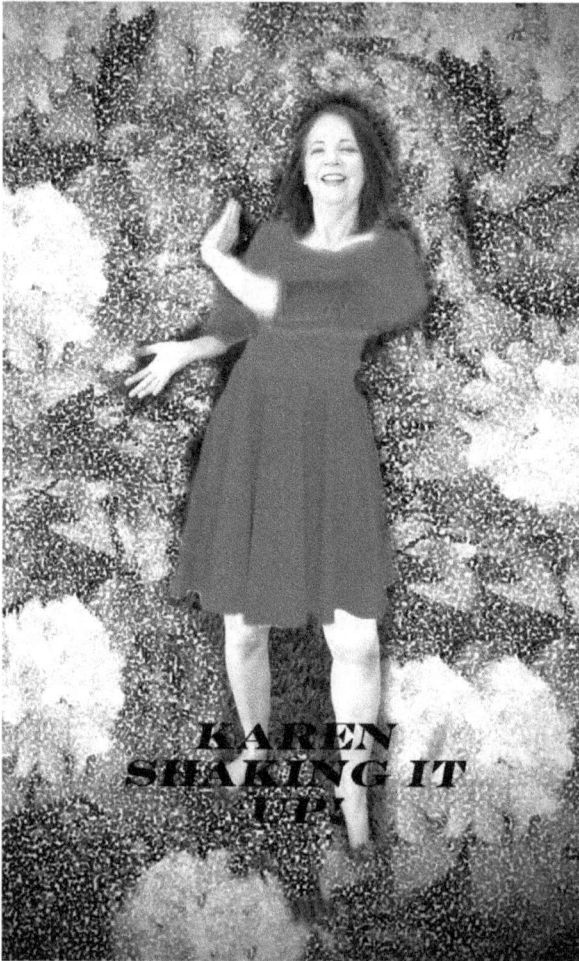

KAREN
SHAKING IT
UP!

Shake it Out!

Time to shake it out,

shake out those in the dump blues.

Time to shake it out,

fill you some big girl shoes.

Time to shake it out,

find you some up close clues.

You know that you paid your dues.

You know stuff that you can use.

So just read some Dr. Seuss,

get out there and vamoose!

Shake it out girl!

Running for Your Life

Red headed, again--

I change back into my alter ego.

I was convinced I needed to go

in that blond direction. You know the one,

where you lighten the gray with highlights, and

keep going with it.

But, somehow it just isn't that time, yet.

With the outer trappings of the new "do,"

I felt like an imposter.

Although, I've felt like a stranger in a strange skin,

for some time, now!

60 is coming, and so is the aging fairy.

I've been feeling her stalking me recently,

making me forget things, encouraging me

to eat more, deepening the lines

on my face. The bitch has it in for me—

I'm telling you!

I've got to get my mojo running,

start training harder and tighten up,

if I'm going to keep a step ahead of this process.

So, I'm putting on my running shoes, and off I go!

Are you with me, ladies?

Here we go, now, run—

RUN for your lives!

ANGELS DO EXIST!
DEMONSTRATED
BY TERRY!

Do You Hear Voices?

Who will go there, if not you?

When the universe chooses and gives you an idea,

will you refuse it,

let it escape you?

Think about it.

Your chance of a lifetime

may have eluded you, or you may have eluded it.

It is your choice to pursue.

If you are true to your innermost self,

you must answer when the

angel whispers in your ear, and says

"You can do it!" Believe!

(With thanks to Sarah Ban Breathnach).

I Dreamed a Dream

I have always upheld

the great American Dream, where

you can be whoever

you want to be.

I am aware that I was held back,

by my shyness, cowardice,

or fear of failing.

I still think that one

has to believe in their dream.

I know many of us won't make it,

however, it is imperative we try.

We must trust what's in our hearts, and

empower these desires.

If we never try,

we have already failed.

ADD + OCD=ODD?

I think I have the attention span,

of a unicellular organism, squashed under

a lens-cover on a slide--I'm easily distracted.

Yes, I'm a little ADD-- just part of my charm!

Communicating with me can be rather like

having a conversation with a squirrel;

I do not sit still for long, never have, never will!

Unless, I'm engaged in OCD behavior,

like searching the Web for some item,

or working in Photoshop; I can get lost for hours

in thousands of images, photo effects, or sites

from the world of on-line shopping.

Wait, is too much sitting making my butt flat?

OMG!

SHERRI CLAIMING
HER TREASURE

Buried Treasure

Sometimes things happen in our lives,

we put ourselves in time-out,

to avoid dealing with our personal demons,

only to find that we cannot get unstuck from there.

We talk about doing something about it,

we just find it easier to stay in our safe haven

of denial, for we have jumped ship.

So, we turn on the TV, or read something trivial,

but we do not grow or move on,

remaining stuck in limbo for days, months, or years.

I would like to offer you some profound advice,

but, I can only give you clues to the treasure you seek.

Start with silence, or quiet music,

to help you hear your voice.

Next, unearth yourself by getting creative.

Dance, paint, cook, or garden—do something you love!

Then, all-hands-on deck! Count your blessings,

talk to friends and give yourself some love.

Repeat often, and never stop!

We are seeking buried treasure mateys!

Don't let your ship sail without you;

stay at your helm and steer true,

with your heart as your one true guide.

Sail on!

Mind Maintenance

Can I have a little quietsy, please?

I need to hear what my body and mind

are trying to tell me,

and I can't hear over your constant

chatter, and the hum of power tools!

Just give me an hour or two of silence,

enough time for me to give myself

a brain root canal, and get the sludge out

that's slowing down my thought processes.

Can I hear me now?

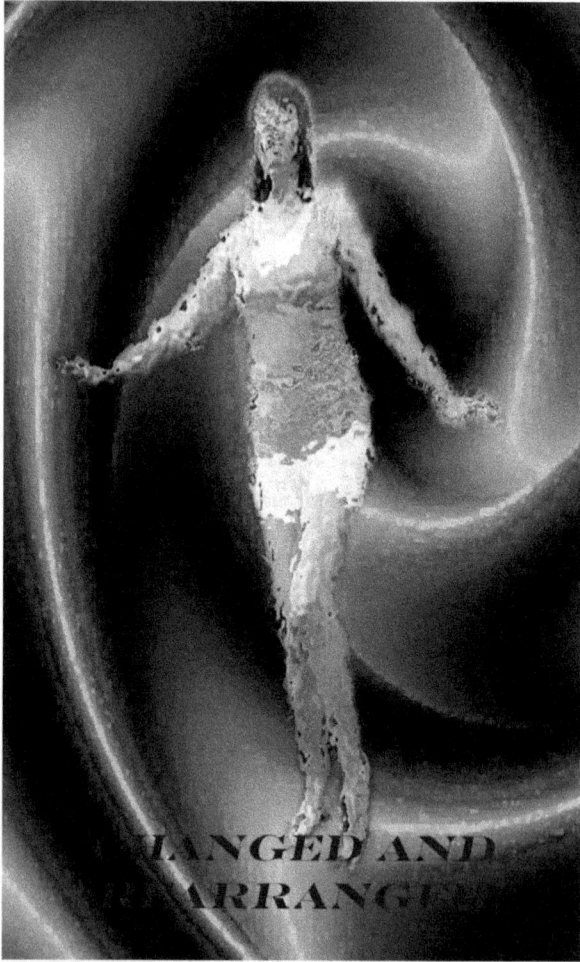

Loving the Stranger Within

So how do I come to accept and love

this somewhat changed and rearranged self?

First, I have to spend some one on one time,

get to know the old/new girl, learn what inspires her.

Secondly, I must exercise self-love; no matter what,

it is still my body, my flesh.

This is how I look and it's **fine**

Aging is not the adversary we think it is.

The enemy is our culture; we must change this,

and pass the truth on to our daughters.

The revelation is that women are beautiful at any age;

we always were, we always will be!

With hearts and eyes wide open,

go forward, have courage, be women!

KAREN
ROOTBOUND!

The Root of the Problem

It has been suggested

that when your life seems without joy

or laughter, and you have no interests,

you may be root-bound and need repotting!

What I take away from this,

is the need to nourish the soul, our roots,

to improve our condition. Subject our foliage

to sunshine, or to the warmth of human touch,

and give our bodies, our plants, sustenance.

To strengthen and green-up, expose ourselves to

fresh air, drink clean water, mist our outer leaves.

Don't forget to feed our heads with

literature, music and friendship.

Then, may we blossom and reach toward the sun!

Spring Weeding

As women, we may tidy up our homes, however,

sometimes we need to do a little spring cleaning, of sorts,

within our lives, weeding out what is no longer useful,

or meaningful for us.

Perhaps we have outgrown a job or a relationship, and

need to find a way to move past this bump in the road,

or brainstorm to reconnect with what we find precious.

In either case, if we don't get down in the dirt

and weed out what is bothering us, we will not thrive.

Don't wait until your life is so choked with hubris

that you become buried alive.

Get out there today and dig it, got it?

Good!

Lighten Up!

May I ask, have you forgiven yourself, lately,

for all things real or imagined,

for your transgressions, your thoughts

against yourself, against others?

Take yourself to task, look inside

and be gentle with what you may find.

Put these "sins" behind you and embrace your life,

your blessings, with a heart full of love.

Know that there are angels surrounding you,

cheering you on, lifting you up.

Let in your light,

and you will "lighten up!"

CPR for Writer's Block

These have been some dry months,

and I'm talking about writing, not drinking.

I'm very good at coming up with excuses not to work,

and I know I want to write.

I think at some level, I had regressed to the point

where I didn't think I had anything left to offer others,

and that is such bull ____!

We should never talk to ourselves this way;

one always has something to offer someone else.

We just have to find the right connections.

Not like the attachments on those defibrillators

to restart our hearts, but the connections of those

who believe in you and your work, without expecting

that you need to give something back.

But, you do want to give back the best of yourself,

to bless them, honor these wonderful friends and family.

These people are your CPR.

They will breathe their hope and love into your heart,

and you will awaken, move forward and live your joy.

It's never too late to rewrite the novel

of your life--ignore the critics.

Believe in yourself.

THE END and

THE BEGINNING!

MARION REBORN

Rebirth

The excavation begun, no longer able to resist

digging into long buried truths from years gone by,

the seal broken on memories that have been

moldering and mildewing, lying in staleness,

internal windows nailed shut.

Somewhere within is born determination

to uncover the mystery and solve the puzzle of self.

Eyelashes flutter then burst open as internal awareness

explodes, lungs gasp with knowledge.

You remember who you are, and

that you are perfect, your inner being

reborn, lily white, blessed,

aglow with love.

Yer Cheatin' Heart

I want to write a novel

with a scintillating story capturing the reader,

transfixing them with the Country and Western

tale of my life.

Featuring: rotten men, cheatin' hearts, and crazy tales

of the 70's, and the usual sex, drugs and rock and roll.

Free love abounded, the reality being

we were exploited with our mini-skirts, etc.,

Candy-land for men.

The abnormal became ever so normal.

It took a decade for all of that to recede, somewhat.

Hippies turned into yuppies, eventually selling out

to the people that they were protesting.

55

The dream of world peace nearly forgotten.

Relative stability crept into my life;

my wilder side tamed or submerged.

Still, we laugh about those days

amazed that we survived them,

our inglorious, glory days

JOAN PACIFIED!

The Pacifier

I have been given a special gift of time.

Most of which I have squandered, although

in my defense, I have been mentioned in *Housekeeping*

Beautiful for keeping up with the housework and laundry!

As much as I want to take time and write,

the process itself means stealing alone time,

which, unfortunately, society has dictated as selfish.

I usually try to juggle work and pleasure—

dusting and vacuuming between commercials,

thereby assuaging the guilt of a little bit of fun.

And how I love to watch chick-flicks,

re-watching some of them over and over.

I have my favorites; it has been a long love affair with TV.

58

It's been a friend or companion when I am in need,

and the background chatter means that I am not alone.

It is so ironic that I need quiet to write,

yet, I constantly fill that silence with noise,

which must just be a pacifier for me.

Hey, perhaps I should suck my thumb instead?

There's a stroke of brilliance, do you think it could work?

A Gift of Kindness

Will you, when being kind to strangers,

save a little kindness for yourself?

So often we do not include ourselves,

yet honor or help our neighbors, or strangers.

What a wonderful thing to cultivate,

giving hope to others and giving it to ourselves.

Remember that we are also deserving

of acts of charity and love, thus ensuring

that we are the gift that keeps on giving.

You Know You Want It!

Hey my sisters

can you come out to play?

Yes, I'm talking to you;

don't you tell me "no way!"

Leave that laundry in the washer,

what do you say?

Life is passing us by,

literally, day by day.

Yes, you can, and yes you may,

have that girlfriend time today!

Can we have an "amen?"

Safe?

What are you willing to do

to keep your secure lifestyle "safe."

Do you go against what you believe in;

compromise your high morals,

and keep your "Daddy" fat and happy,

to enable living off the hand that feeds?

Do you watch your tongue

so, there is no back talk,

and no repercussions?

Your alternative, some kind of poverty

versus the dearth of a creative wasteland?

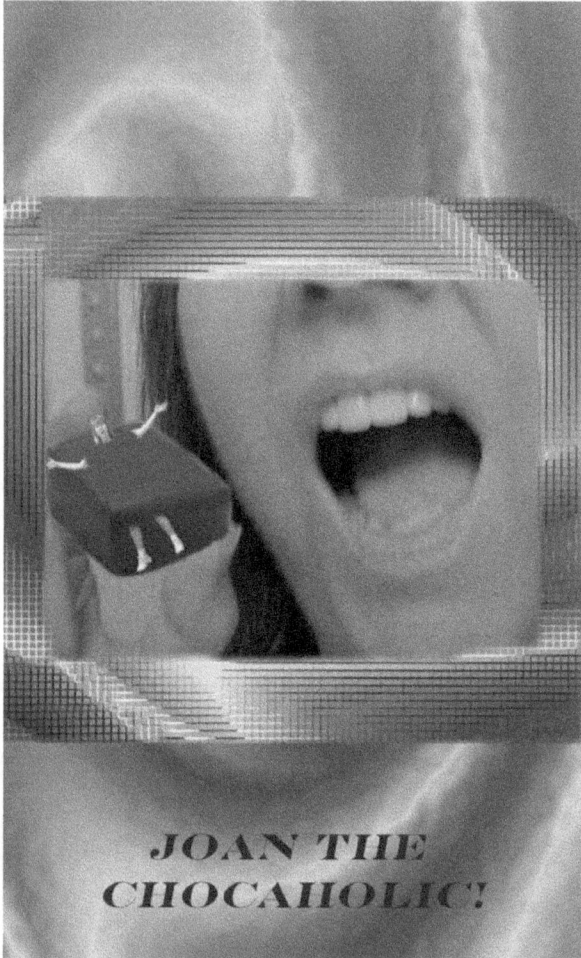

JOAN THE
CHOCAHOLIC!

I Must Confess; I'm a Chocoholic, Yes!

Don't lie there with that innocent look.

I can see where this is going,

I could write a book!

So flirtatious, striking a pose;

all that chocolate hanging out,

temptingly, anything goes!

My" dark" secret a shock;

easily seduced, a willing participant,

I'll just turn the lock!

My Freudian Slip Is Showing!

If writing is therapy, then I've been

standing up my shrink, for some time!

My fixations are simple, broken down into two things:

I want to lose weight and I must have chocolate.

Now is that a conflict of interest?

But getting back to that writing thing,

it can be easy at times, words

flowing from my pen like water from a font.

Usually my attempts to write

are like trying to cross a river in a leaky boat.

I start out, I sink; I go back to the start.

65

But my best work involves distraction, the art of

subjugating my true desire with anything else,

to prevent picking up the pen.

Essentially, I have a master's degree in

the Ostrich Technique—perhaps you've heard of it?

Hmmm?

With Leaded Feet

A decade after the big 5-0,

after an initial high energy sprint, I find

I have been walking in circles, for the past few years.

Apparently, I have been trampling over plans and dreams,

I should have carried out; I have been holding "me" back,

with the usual fear of failing, or flying, like Erica Jong.

Even though I'm not usually aware of this,

the truth lies under the surface,

like ground water moving silently beneath me.

Acknowledging that I am wrong, armed with

friends and support, I stumble forward on a new path.

It is rocky, full of potholes, and uphill, but

this is my path, no-one else's, I chose it so, **HERE I GO!**

JOAN AFLAME!

Aflame

Have you discovered that

you are not alone in this world?

Humans cannot exist on this planet as an island of one.

And, have you found your

Higher Power, Spirit, God, or

whatever you choose to call him/her/it?

Have you plugged your "adaptor"

into this power source, and experienced

enlightenment, and/or a power surge?

We must believe that our existence

is much more than just that.

Find what ignites your heart of hearts,

be drawn in like moth to flame.

Glow with inner fire; life will never be the same!

A Woman for All Ages

Here is a shock for you,

not all of us are moms who do it all,

or are executives, who crashed the glass ceiling,

left, and found their true calling.

Some of us have just been trying to make a living,

worker bees who buried creative or other needs,

like self-expression, under a load of work and life.

It happens, and time passes.

I swallowed the work ethic myth hook, line and

sinker. The "perfect" employee—hard working,

taking a personal interest in my job.

My Mary Poppins' era; but, it left nothing for me.

50 opened up my eyes.

I still work hard, but now I work for me.

71

First and foremost, I take care of myself

and my responsibilities to family.

As time passes, we need to deal with

and understand, what lessons each decade teaches us.

Hopefully we learn and embrace the wisdom

from our experiences, and in turn,

these life lessons flesh out

who we are becoming, and who we grow to be.

We are unfinished works of art,

the book not yet completed,

the half-carved sculpture,

to be unveiled by the universe,

and not at a time of our choosing.

Let the journey unfold, and may your story be told!

About the Author

Joan Ellen Gage, a farmer's daughter hailing from the Finger Lakes area in New York, moved with her family to south Florida as a teenager and spent the lion's share of her life there. She now resides in Western North Carolina.

Joan is a writer of poetry, women's humor and inspiration with a spotlight on the midlife experience. Ms. Gage aspires to be a cheerleader for women of all ages, and published *Embracing Your Inner Cheerleader,* in 2012. Joan is also the author of *Water Running Downhill, Words of Empowerment for Women in Midlife*, which was published in 2007, and *Stranger in a Strange Skin*, published in 2011, which is only available as an eBook.

Ms. Gage is a dabbler in photography, who infuses her photo-creations with humor and special effects. Additionally, Joan relishes writing blogs for women and more, at: www.joanellengage.com and at: https://joanszoneblogalicious.wordpress.com/. Click in to get your hip chick wit!